COOL CARS
FORD
MUSTANG
DARK HORSE
EPIC
BY KAITLYN DULING
BELLWETHER MEDIA ››› MINNEAPOLIS, MN

EPIC BOOKS are no ordinary books. They burst with intense action, high-speed heroics, and shadows of the unknown. Are you ready for an Epic adventure?

This edition first published in 2025 by Bellwether Media, Inc.

Library of Congress Cataloging-in-Publication Data

LC record for Ford Mustang Dark Horse available at: https://lccn.loc.gov/2024039177

Editor: Rachael Barnes Designer: Gabriel Hilger

Printed in the United States of America, North Mankato, MN.

TABLE OF CONTENTS

SPINNING OUT

Two Ford Mustang Dark Horse engines roar. The drivers hit the gas with Line Lock on. Only the back wheels spin.

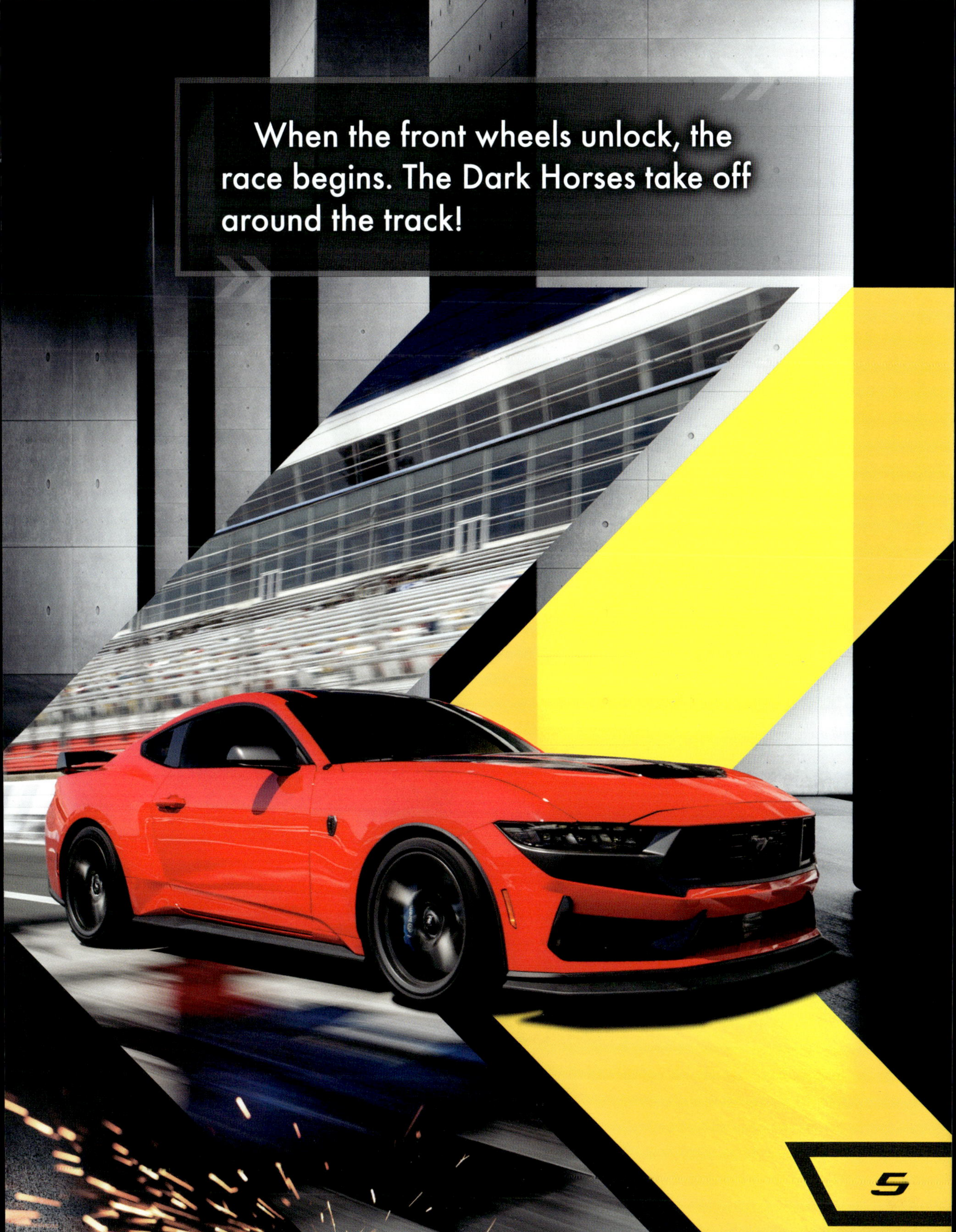

When the front wheels unlock, the race begins. The Dark Horses take off around the track!

ALL ABOUT THE DARK HORSE

HENRY FORD

1964 FORD MUSTANG

Henry Ford started the Ford Motor Company in Michigan in 1903. The first Ford Mustang was sold in 1964.

Just like the first Mustang **model**, the Dark Horse is known for its powerful **V8 engine**.

2022 DARK HORSE V8 ENGINE

WHERE IS IT MADE?

The Dark Horse is a Mustang **variant**. It is built like the Mustang Mach 1.

The Dark Horse looks tough and drives fast. It is one powerful Mustang!

2024 DARK HORSE

DARK HORSE BASICS

YEAR FIRST MADE	2024
COST	starting at $63,280
HOW MANY MADE	currently in production

FEATURES

front grille

hood vent

spoiler

The Dark Horse is meant for the road. The Dark Horse S and Dark Horse R are built to race.

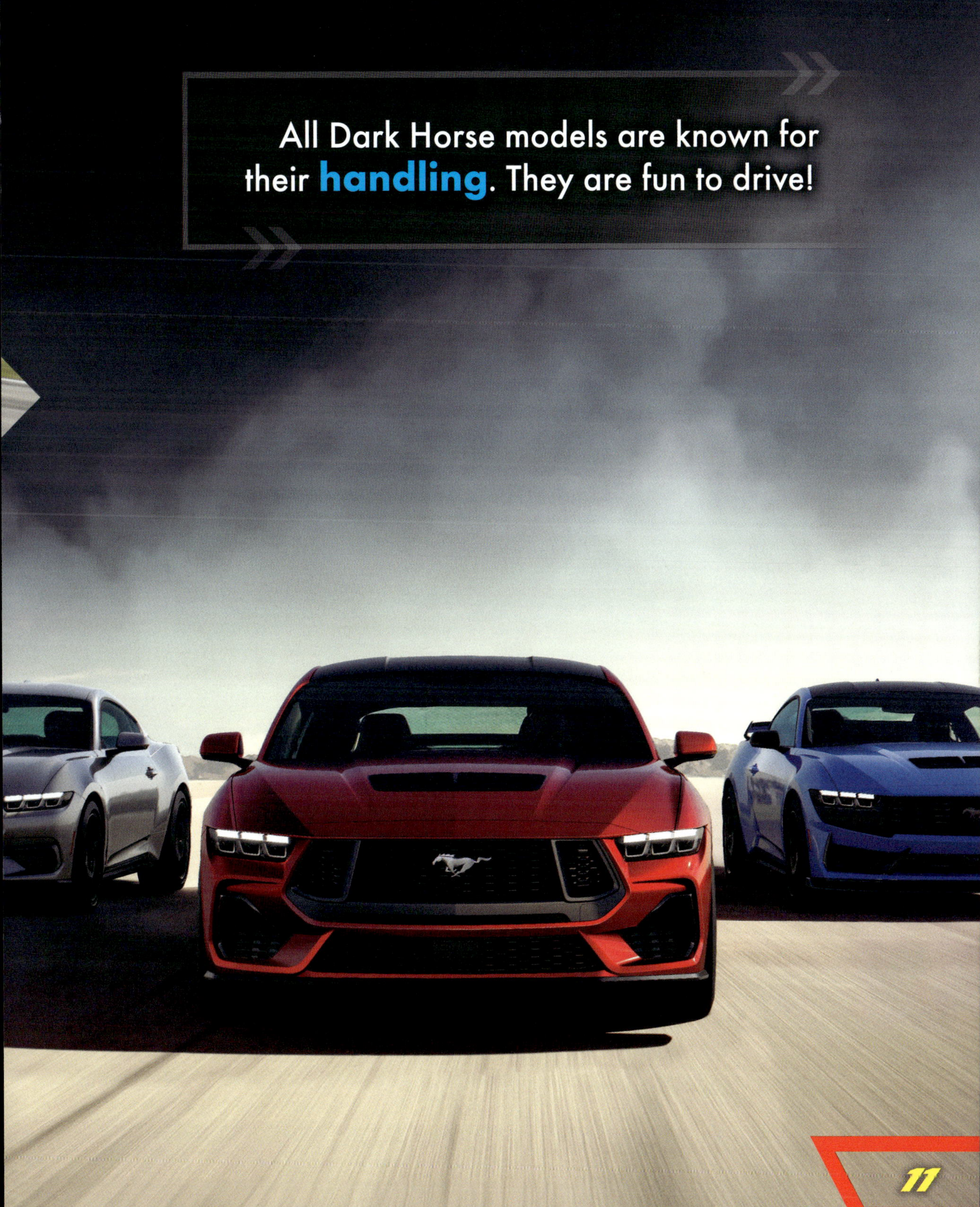

All Dark Horse models are known for their **handling**. They are fun to drive!

PARTS OF THE DARK HORSE

The Dark Horse can have a **manual transmission**. This allows the car to reach 60 miles (97 kilometers) per hour in 4.1 seconds.

With an **automatic transmission**, the 0-to-60 time is 3.7 seconds!

ENGINE SPECS

V8 ENGINE

TOP SPEED	166 miles (267 kilometers) per hour
0-60 TIME	as low as 3.7 seconds
HORSEPOWER	500 hp

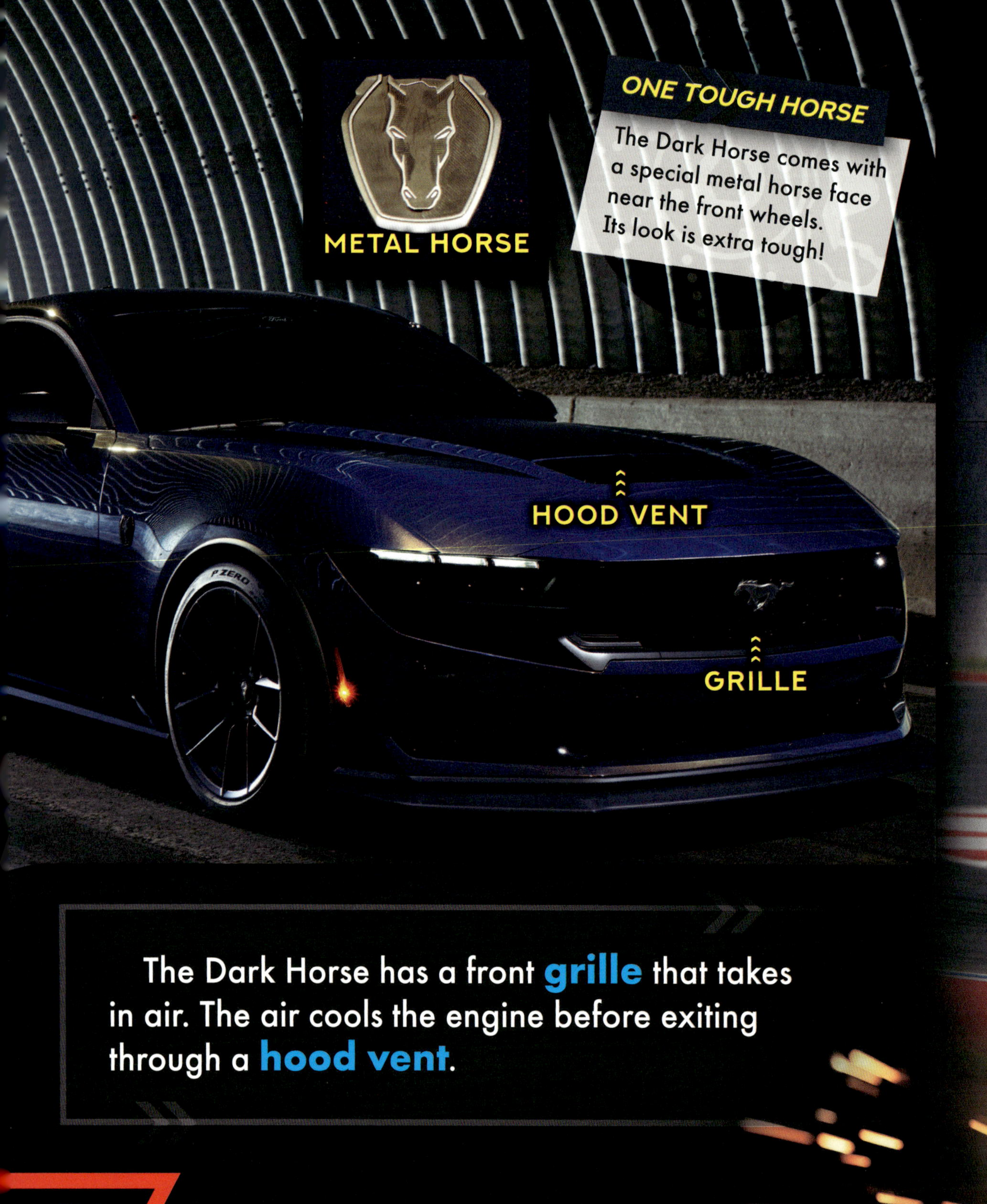

ONE TOUGH HORSE

The Dark Horse comes with a special metal horse face near the front wheels. Its look is extra tough!

The Dark Horse has a front **grille** that takes in air. The air cools the engine before exiting through a **hood vent**.

A rear **spoiler** helps the car grip the road, even at low speeds.

Track Apps records information like speed and driving times.

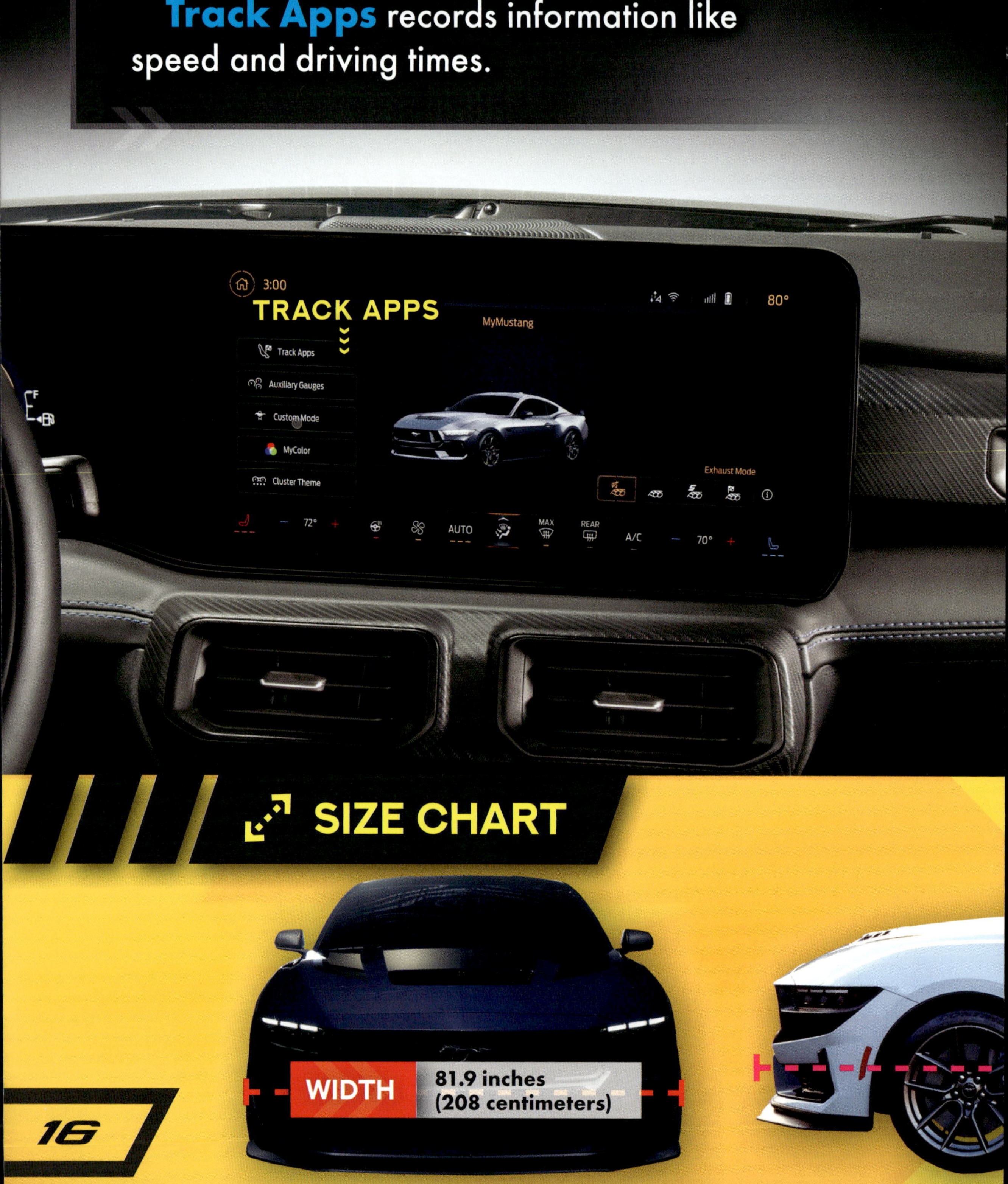

The Line Lock app locks the front wheels. Only the back wheels spin when the driver hits the gas! The warm back tires get better grip.

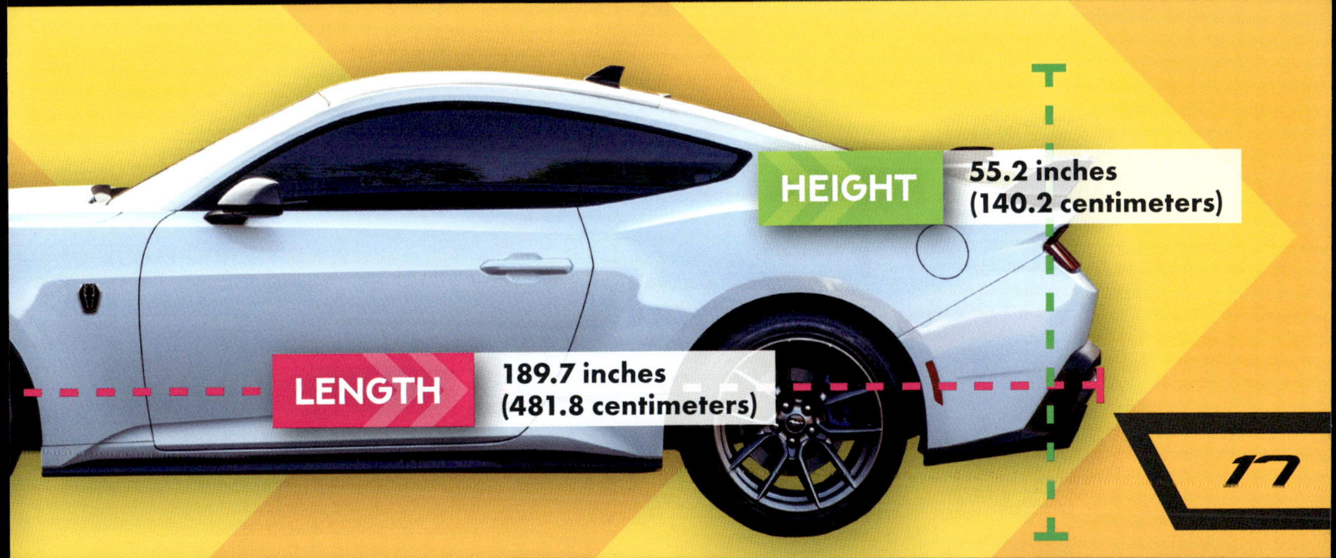

HEIGHT 55.2 inches (140.2 centimeters)

LENGTH 189.7 inches (481.8 centimeters)

Drivers can **rev** the Dark Horse's engine from outside the car. They press a button on the **key fob**.

NEW COLOR, NEW LOOK

Ford made a new paint color just for the Dark Horse. The car can come in a color-shifting blue!

FRONT SEATS

The Dark Horse Premium adds comfort features like cooled front seats.

THE DARK HORSE'S FUTURE

The popular Dark Horse model is still being made. Ford will keep building other Mustangs, too.

The Mustang GTD hit the road in 2025. It reaches up to 800 **horsepower**. Fans continue to enjoy fast and powerful Mustangs!

IN HONOR OF

A special Mustang released in 2025 honors the 1965 Mustang. Only 1,965 will be made.

MUSTANG GTD

GLOSSARY

automatic transmission—a car system that shifts gears for the driver

grille—a set of bars that covers an opening on the front of a car; the grille allows air to enter and exit the engine.

handling—how a car performs around turns

hood vent—an opening in a car's hood that allows air to exit

horsepower—a measurement of the power of an engine or motor

key fob—a small remote used to control some functions of a car

manual transmission—a system that a driver uses to shift gears

model—a specific kind of car

rev—to cause an engine to run more quickly

spoiler—a part on the back of a car that helps the car grip the road

Track Apps—a program downloaded onto a car system that controls special settings and tracks drive information

V8 engine—an engine with 8 cylinders arranged in the shape of a "V"

variant—a model that is closely related to but notably different from the base model

TO LEARN MORE

AT THE LIBRARY

Duling, Kaitlyn. *Ford Mustang Shelby GT500*. Minneapolis, Minn.: Bellwether Media, 2025.

Emminizer, Theresa. *Mustangs*. Buffalo, N.Y.: Enslow Publishing, 2023.

James, Ryan. *Muscle Cars*. Coral Springs, Fla.: Seahorse Publishing, 2022.

ON THE WEB

FACTSURFER

Factsurfer.com gives you a safe, fun way to find more information.

1. Go to www.factsurfer.com.
2. Enter "Ford Mustang Dark Horse" into the search box and click 🔍.
3. Select your book cover to see a list of related content.

INDEX

The images in this book are reproduced through the courtesy of: Ford, front cover, pp. 3, 4, 5, 7, 8, 9 (isolated Mustang, front grille, hood vent, spoiler), 10, 11, 12, 13, 14 (Mustang Dark Horse), 15, 16 (Track Apps, width), 17 (main, length), 19, 20; Classic-Ads/ Alamy, p. 6 (1964 Ford Mustang); Sueddeutsche Zeitung Photo/ Alamy, p. 6 (Henry Ford); Vehicles/ Alamy, p. 14 (metal horse); Bloomberg/ Contributor/ Getty Images, p. 18; Jack Skeens, p. 21.